T 74901

W9-APH-469

Paul Kariya

ANDREW
PODNIEKS

WITHDRAWN FROM
FORT WORTH COUNTRY DAY SCHOOL

GREYSTONE BOOKS
Douglas & McIntyre
Vancouver/Toronto/New York

Fort Worth Country Day School Library
4200 Country Day Lane
Fort Worth, Texas 76109

Text copyright © 2000 by Andrew Podnieks

00 01 02 03 04   5 4 3 2 1

All rights reserved. No part of this book may be reproduced, stored in a retrieval system or transmitted in any form or by any means, without the prior permission of the publisher or, in the case of photocopying or other reprographic copying, a license from CANCOPY (Canadian Reprography Collective), Toronto, Ontario.

Greystone Books
A division of Douglas & McIntyre Ltd.
2323 Quebec Street, Suite 201
Vancouver, British Columbia
Canada V5T 4S7

Canadian Cataloguing in Publication Data
Podnieks, Andrew
    Paul Kariya
    (Hockey heroes)
    ISBN 1-55054-792-5
    1. Kariya, Paul, 1974– —Juvenile literature.
2. Hockey players—Biography—Juvenile literature.
I. Title. II. Series: Hockey heroes (Vancouver, B.C.)
GV848.5.K37P62 2000   j796.962′092   C00-910161-6

Editing by Michael Carroll
Cover and text design by Peter Cocking
Front cover photograph by Bruce Bennett/Bruce Bennett Studios
Back cover photograph by Henry DiRocco/Bruce Bennett Studios
Printed and bound in Hong Kong by C&C Offset Printing Co. Ltd.
Printed on acid-free paper ∞

Every reasonable care has been taken to trace the ownership of copyrighted visual material. Information that will enable the publisher to rectify any reference or credit is welcome.

All NHL logos and marks and team logos and marks depicted herein are the property of the NHL and the respective teams and may not be reproduced without the prior written consent of NHL Enterprises, Inc. © 2000 NHL.

The publisher gratefully acknowledges the assistance of the Canada Council for the Arts and of the British Columbia Ministry of Tourism, Small Business and Culture. The publisher also acknowledges the financial support of the Government of Canada through the Book Publishing Industry Development Program (BPIDP) for its publishing activities.

Photo credits

Photos by Bruce Bennett Studios:
pp. i (center left), iv, 3, 18, 23, 24, 37: Bruce Bennett
pp. i (center right), 21, 38: Brian Winkler
pp. i (bottom), 42: John Tremmel
pp. iii, 31: John Giamundo
p. 4: Mark Hicks
pp. 6, 27, 34: Art Foxall
pp. 9, 28, 32: Henry DiRocco
p. 13: Scott Levy
p. 41: Jim Leary

Photos on pp. i (top), 10, 14, 16, 17 by Monty Rand

Although he lacked

confidence in his shot

when he entered the NHL,

Paul has one of the best

slap shots in the league.

CHAPTER ONE

Shooting for the Top

Paul Kariya was about 10 years old when he first saw Wayne Gretzky play hockey in person. The Great One was in Vancouver with the Edmonton Oilers, so Paul's parents took him to see his hero play the Canucks. "He was my idol," Paul later said, remembering that night. "I was the only one cheering."

Just like Gretzky, Paul first began skating when he was three years old. He wasn't very good. He had weak ankles, and everyone at school made fun of him because he took figure-skating, not hockey, lessons. His classmates said he skated like a girl. But Paul didn't care. He loved to slide along the ice. He loved the cool feeling of speed and wind. The more he skated, the better he became. By the time he was five, he had joined his first hockey team.

Paul also played other sports such as golf, lacrosse, rugby, tennis and basketball. Each sport made him happy, even if he was only using a folded-up sock as a baseball, or a soup can for a golf hole. All of these activities helped Paul to develop quick reflexes that he could use in hockey. This gave him an advantage over many of his schoolmates.

When Paul was growing up in Vancouver, sports were always second to his family in importance. His parents were Japanese, and they wanted their children to be interested in that culture. Paul and his sister, Michiko, went to a Japanese-language school as well as to an English school. "I'm very proud of my Japanese heritage," Paul declares now. But as he got older, his love for hockey became more important than his Japanese classes. "We weren't pushed," he says. "If you didn't want to learn Japanese, fine."

Paul has a hundred moves to fool a goalie.

Although he has always been proud of being Canadian, his family's background is also important. For instance, each of the five Kariya children has a Canadian and a Japanese name. Paul's full name is Paul Tetsuhiko Kariya.

As Paul got a little older, he started watching hockey games on television. He loved Wayne Gretzky, and even tried to skate like the Great One, bent over at the waist almost as if he were

trying to hide on the ice. By the time Paul was nine, he was already playing Peewee with 14-year-olds. At his house he went out to the backyard to a woodshed that had holes in it. He put pucks down in front of the shed on a piece of old fiberglass that he got from a nearby hockey arena. Then he tried to shoot the pucks through the holes. That was how he practiced his shot.

Although Paul's parents encouraged their children to play sports, they believed education was more important. As a result, studying always came before playing in the Kariya home. Paul attended Argyle Secondary School in Vancouver, where his father taught mathematics and computer science. And Paul's mother was also a teacher.

By the time Paul was a teenager, he had more or less given up other sports so he could play hockey. The Canadian Amateur Hockey Association had a special program for talented young players. It was called the Program of Excellence, and the coaches asked Paul to play for their under-17 team, even though he was only 15. The next year Paul traveled with the team to Japan to take part in the Phoenix Cup tournament. He was the top scorer and was named to the all-star team. He now knew hockey was in his blood.

After returning to Canada, Paul had another great chance. The British Columbia Junior Hockey League (BCJHL) was expanding to include a team in Penticton, a town about 120 miles (200 kilometers) from Vancouver. One day the coach of that new team, Garry Davidson, came to watch Paul play. "He was even better than I'd heard" was all Davidson could say. He hoped he could convince Paul to join his new team.

Because Penticton had a good school and the hockey program was yearlong, Paul's parents agreed to let him move to the new town that fall to play in the BCJHL. Paul boarded with the Stork family in Penticton and tried out for the Penticton Panthers. There were 170 skaters at tryouts, but the coach was allowed to choose only 22 players. At 16, Paul was the youngest at camp. Most of the others were 18.

Amazing Atom

When Paul Kariya was very young, he moved from Tyke to Novice and then to Atom hockey faster than most children. Three leagues in three years was a pretty big jump. In Atom, Paul's dad was the coach. "Paul liked to set up plays," Mr. Kariya recalls. "I told him, 'The puck is there, you move it, keep it moving.' That's something we stressed to all our kids—to share."

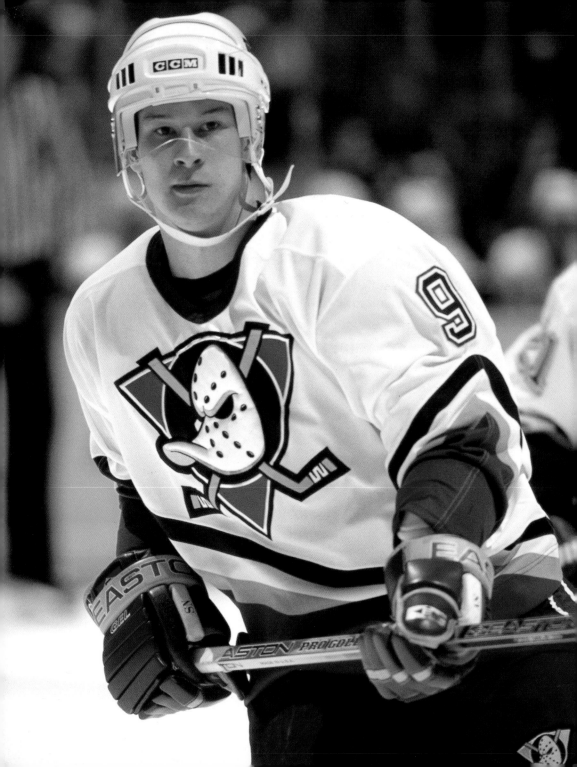

Not only did Paul make the team, he was the best player there and coach Davidson named him team captain.

Paul was happy in Penticton. He played hockey with skilled players, and he learned how to skate alongside much bigger young men. In his first season, the team finished last in the standings and won only 11 times. Paul had 112 points in just 60 games and was named the league's most sportsmanlike player for his gentlemanly conduct on ice.

The young Panther quickly became famous. Scouts from other teams and leagues made special trips to Penticton just to watch him play. The Victoria Cougars of the Western Hockey League asked Paul to play for them, but he was content where he was. He studied hard, and when he wasn't playing or practicing, he read books. He also followed a strict diet. He refused to eat anything other than pasta, fruit, salads and some protein. A few people thought he was crazy, but he had an answer ready for them: "You have to set a goal and focus."

Paul's second year with the Panthers was a dream come true. He scored and set up goals the way he had the year before, but now the team won. Then, in early December, he got a

THE PAUL KARIYA FILE

Position: Left wing

Born: October 16, 1974, Vancouver, Canada

Height: Five feet eleven inches (1.8 meters)

Weight: 180 pounds (82 kilograms)

Shoots: Left

Number: 9

Favorite Food: Seafood

Hobbies: Juggling, reading

Favorite Actor: Robert De Niro

Off-Season Sports: Golf, tennis

Childhood Hockey Hero: Wayne Gretzky

Hockey Highlight: 1994 Olympics

phone call that changed his life. Coach Rick Cornaccia of the Canadian National Junior Team called to tell him he had been selected to play for Canada at the World Junior Championships in Germany. Paul was never more excited in his life. He was just 17 years old and would be traveling to Europe to play for his country. And one of his teammates would be Eric Lindros!

Canada finished in sixth place at the 1992 World Junior Championships. That was disappointing, but Paul scored a goal for Canada. He became good friends with Lindros and learned a lot from him. When he returned to Penticton, he was exhausted and should have taken a break. But Paul wanted to represent the Panthers in the all-star game the league held every year. When he got to Victoria, British Columbia, to play, he collapsed in the hotel lobby. The doctor told him to rest because he had mononucleosis, a sickness that makes a person really tired.

As a superstar, Paul takes more than his share of hits.

Paul missed the next 12 games for Penticton. But he was still so good that he scored 132 points in just 40 games, an average of more than three points a game. He was selected the most valuable player in all of Canada and was again chosen the most gentlemanly player, as well. Every time he skated, he came off the ice a better player. Every move he made, he moved just a little faster. He was training hard to be the best player he could be, but he knew there was so much more he could improve.

It was time to move on.

A team leader even as

a teenager, Paul captained

the University of Maine

to a U.S. championship in

his last season.

CHAPTER TWO

Black Bears Rule

While playing for Penticton, Paul had proven to himself that he was a better player than he had thought. At the end of his second year with the Panthers, he had a tough decision to make about where he was going to play next. He could stay at Penticton, he could play in the Canadian junior leagues or he could go to university or college and pursue an education as well as a hockey career.

He decided on college in the United States because he could continue to attend classes and still play hockey at a high level. He chose the University of Maine because the city of Orono, where the campus was located, reminded him a lot of Penticton, except that it was colder.

When Paul arrived at the Alfond Arena in Orono for his first practice, he knew a great challenge lay ahead. In 1987 Maine had become a member of Division I hockey, the highest level in American college competition. But the school had never won a national championship because the Black Bears were in a division called Hockey East. Nine of the best teams in the country were in this division.

The Black Bears went undefeated through the first half of the season, and Paul was by far the best player on the team. Scouts started comparing him to Wayne Gretzky because of his incredible passing ability. Even when opponents expected him to pass, he still got the puck to the man he was looking for. "In my brain, I'm saying pass first, shoot second," Paul reveals. "Sometimes that gets me in trouble, but I like to think that 99 per cent of the time the pass is the right play." In December the Black Bears were invited to the Great Alaska Face-Off Tournament in Fairbanks, Alaska. The Black Bears won all three games, and Paul was named most valuable player.

Paul shone at the 1993 World Junior Championships.

Then came the winter holidays. Everyone else at Maine went back to their families for Christmas. But Paul was invited to represent Canada at the 1993 World Junior Championships, this time in Sweden. He was amazing, and Canada won a

gold medal. Paul had two goals and eight points in the seven games Canada played. Again he was named best player in the tournament.

Paul returned to Maine a hero, and scouts were now saying he was the best young hockey player in the world. He quickly put on his powder-blue Maine sweater again, and the Black Bears kept on winning. They beat Boston University 5–2 to win the Hockey East championship, then eliminated Minnesota and Michigan to make it to the college finals for the first time.

The finals were a celebration of the entire U.S. college season. Before the championship game—Maine versus Lake Superior—there was an awards night for all the players. This turned out to be the most important evening of Paul's life. He was given the Hobey Baker Award as the best player in U.S. college hockey. A first-year student had never won the award before.

There was still the championship game against Lake Superior to play. In the first period, the Black Bears went ahead 2–0, but by the end of the second, they were behind 4–2. "I looked down the bench and I was afraid that my players were going to lose their composure," coach Shawn Walsh said about his players early in the third period. "But I saw Paul leading the team in deep-breathing exercises, telling the guys on the bench to concentrate on the basics."

With Paul the "basics" are simple. When Paul has the puck, skate to open ice and he will pass it. Whenever possible, go to the net. That's where all goals are scored, after all.

Early in the third period of the college championship game, Paul made a beautiful pass across the crease to Jim Montgomery. The pass fooled the goaltender, and Montgomery tapped the puck into the open side of the net. The score was now 4–3.

A few minutes later Paul started another pretty passing play that also ended in a goal for Maine. The score was now 4–4. A couple of shifts later Paul skated down the left wing and made a beautiful deke around a surprised Lake Superior defenseman. He hit Montgomery with another perfect pass right at the goalmouth. Again the puck was in the net. Three incredible passes by Paul! The Bears held on to win 5–4 and became college champions.

In the dressing room after the victory, Paul praised his teammates. "My linemates aren't just my line-mates," he said. "They're my best friends. The fact that we came back and did it together is just amazing. If I never play another hockey game, this would be a nice way to end my career."

Sibling Rivalry

There is nothing like a little family rivalry to keep hockey fun. Paul Kariya's younger brother, Steve, also plays hockey. He, too, went to the University of Maine, and in the fall of 1999 he made the Vancouver Canucks. But Steve wears number 18 because, he says with a competitive smile, "I'll be twice as good as my brother."

Never play another game? Fat chance. Soon after the
Lake Superior game Paul got another phone call. This time it
was from Mike Keenan, the coach of Canada's national team.
Keenan asked him to join the squad in Germany, where the
World Championships were being held. The World Junior
Championships is a tournament for players who are under

20 years of age. The World Championships is for
older players. Everyone on Team Canada, except
Paul, played in the National Hockey League
(NHL). He was the only one who was in junior-
level hockey. Paul was also the only teenager
on the team and the youngest player ever to
represent Canada at the World Championships.
"He has some of the attributes of Wayne
Gretzky," Keenan explained when asked why
he had chosen Paul.

Although Canada finished fourth at the
World Championships, Paul played on a line with
Mark Recchi and his old friend, Eric Lindros. He
led all Canadian players in scoring and showed Keenan just
how smart it was to invite him. "He is deceptively fast," Keenan
said after watching the young star play for three weeks. "He
seems to be able to anticipate and read plays well, and that
gives him creative space. There are very few people who com-
pare to Gretzky in terms of that."

Paul was 18 years old and about to enter the most important
stage of his career.

HOBEY BAKER MEMORIAL AWARD
[...] TO THE OUTSTANDING COLLEGIATE HOCKEY PL[...]
THE UNITED STATES BY THE
[...]LETIC CLU[...] BLOOMINGTON, MINNESOTA

HEROIC HOBEY BAKER

Although even smaller than Paul Kariya, Hobey Baker was an excellent athlete in football and hockey during his college days at Princeton University from 1910 to 1914. Baker played rover, a position that no longer exists in hockey, and he was famous for his stickhandling. Once he had the puck, players would say you couldn't get it off him. He died in France at the end of World War I. In his honor, the Hobey Baker Award was established for the best college hockey player in the United States.

Paul's number-one goal

was to play for Canada at

the Olympics, a dream that

came true in Lillehammer,

Norway, in 1994.

CHAPTER THREE

Olympic Dreams

Paul had to decide if he was going to return to Maine in the fall. He also had to see if Team Canada would invite him to play at the Olympics in Lillehammer, Norway. That was his dream. And he had to wait for the NHL Entry Draft, because once a player turns 18, he can start to play in the big league. Whichever team selected Paul might want him to begin immediately. He had all sorts of decisions to make. "I can't start making plans for the rest of my career," he said quietly. "I'm not even in the NHL yet."

Mike Penny, the chief scout for the Vancouver Canucks, had full confidence in Paul. "He's a fast skater, has a great shot, is a good scorer and has a good hockey sense. He has a very good character on and off the ice. This young man should have no problem starting on an NHL team."

But Paul was really worried as draft day approached: "A lot of players talked about having met with 16 teams. I only got interviewed by one—Hartford—and it worried me. I thought I might not even get drafted."

As Paul sat in the Quebec City arena the day of the 1993 draft, he was depressed. "It was like a conspiracy," he said. Here he was, the top college player the previous season, yet no NHL team wanted to draft him. "As soon as I got into my seat," Paul admitted, "I remember feeling just totally helpless. For the first time in my life, I had no control over my destiny. I got really nervous and sort of blanked out for a bit."

For the first time, Paul dons a Mighty Ducks jersey.

But there was no devious plan to keep Paul out of the NHL. The Mighty Ducks of Anaheim wanted him so much that instead of talking to him and showing all the other teams how interested they were, they decided to ignore him and pretend they didn't care. But they cared very much.

Anaheim was the fourth team to select at the 1993 draft, so there were three other teams that could have chosen Paul before the Ducks. The Ottawa Senators selected first. They took Alexandre Daigle, who played junior hockey in Quebec.

Hartford came next, and the Whalers chose Chris Pronger. Two down, one to go. Tampa Bay, selecting third, could have chosen Paul. The team's scouts knew he had speed and skill. But the Lightning selected Chris Gratton because he was bigger. Paul was disappointed. Name after name was called, but not his.

Michael Eisner was the chairman of Walt Disney Company, which owned the Mighty Ducks. Eisner jumped for joy when it was Anaheim's turn to choose. He walked up to the podium and announced, "The Mighty Ducks of Anaheim are pleased to select, from the University of Maine, Paul Kariya."

Although Paul was now able to play in the NHL, he still had those other dreams he wanted to fulfill before joining the Mighty Ducks. "I'm a big Wayne Gretzky fan," he reminded everyone, "and in one of his books he wrote, 'The one thing I regret is not being able to play in the Olympics.' If you look at the guy's career, you can understand why it means so much."

Paul wanted to play for the Ducks, but he knew the NHL could wait until after he played for Canada at the Olympics in Lillehammer. First, he returned to Maine for another semester of his business administration degree.

He played just 12 games for the Black Bears, but they were hard ones. "I really pride myself on being a very focused individual. But I

Picture Perfect

For a long time, Paul Kariya has used visualization to prepare for games. He closes his eyes and actually tries to see how the game will take place. He makes moves and passes in his head and figures out how he can help his team. "Hockey is a lot like chess," he says. "You have certain moves that are always repeated, and knowing that, you can plan your next move." That's what visualization is all about—being prepared.

found myself before Maine games thinking about playing in the Olympics," he confessed later. No one was happier when Paul joined the Canadian team than coach Tom Renney: "He's going to bring us offense, speed, winning attitude and outstanding character and class."

By the time the Canadian players arrived in Lillehammer for the Olympics, they had been together for a number of weeks and were ready to earn a medal. In the first game, Paul got an assist on Petr Nedved's opening goal, and Canada beat

Italy 7–2. When he stood at his blueline after the game and heard his country's national anthem, "O Canada," played, he knew this was the experience of a lifetime.

All in all, the Canadians won three games, lost one and tied one in the first round. They then faced the tough Czech Republic team in the quarter finals. The game was tied 2–2 after regulation time, but at 5:54 of overtime Paul scored the winning goal, a beautiful shot right off the faceoff. It was the biggest goal of his career, and it put Canada in the semi-finals against Finland.

The Canadians beat the Finns 5–3, then faced a team from Sweden in the gold-medal final. The Swedes led 1–0 going into the third period, but once more Paul was the hero. He tied the game, then each team scored again before the end of the period, forcing overtime. Neither team scored in the 10-minute period, so a shootout followed.

In a shootout, each team gets five penalty shots. The one with the most goals wins the game. Paul scored in the shootout for Canada, and so did Nedved, but Sweden also scored twice. This led to a sudden-death shoot-out. Each time one team scored, the other had to score also or the game would be over. The tension was incredible. Peter Forsberg scored for Sweden, and Paul was chosen to shoot again for Canada. The gold medal came down to one shot. If Paul scored, the shootout would continue. If he missed, Sweden would win Olympic gold.

It wasn't gold, but Paul was proud of his team's silver medal.

Paul stood at center ice and looked at the puck. Then he glanced at Sweden's goalie, Tommy Salo, hunched over in the crease. Skating in alone, Paul saw Salo move back into his net, so he took a quick wrist shot. Salo was falling down, but he got his pad on the puck and kicked it out. The Canadians were stunned. Sweden had won the gold medal.

Paul was devastated. "I've gone over that penalty shot about 200 times in my head, trying to change it," he said later. "We didn't have high expectations going in. But going all the way and coming so close...it's an empty feeling not having that gold."

Maybe Paul didn't win gold at the Olympics, but just a couple of months later he led Canada to victory in the World Championships in Milan, Italy. This time Paul did every-thing right. The Canadians won all their games in the tourna-ment, and in the semifinals they hammered Sweden 6–0 before defeating Finland to win the gold medal. The win against Sweden was sweet revenge for the gold-medal loss in the Olympics, and Paul was voted the outstanding forward.

Next stop: Anaheim, California.

DISNEY DUCKS

When Anaheim, California, was awarded an NHL franchise for the 1993–94 season, the team was owned by the Walt Disney Company. Michael Eisner, Disney's chairman, named the club the Mighty Ducks after the popular movie about a bunch of not very good young hockey players who win a league championship. It was a "dreams come true" fairy-tale story, and Eisner hoped the same happy ending would happen to his new team.

In his first year in the

NHL, Paul played with the

confidence of a veteran

and earned the respect of

opponents everywhere.

CHAPTER FOUR

Mighty Duck Days

Because of a contract dispute between NHL team owners and players in 1994, Paul's first regular-season game in the league was delayed by months. With plenty of time on his hands, he worked out in a gym to try to get stronger. "Everything I do I want to win at," he said. "When I'm in the gym, from weight training to squats, I want to be the best, even though guys are bigger than me. I want to be the best in everything. The same on the ice. Winning is so sweet, and it is such a rush when you know your team is the best and you are part of that."

Paul gained six pounds in just a few weeks, and when the 1994–95 season finally started, he was stronger than ever. Now it was time to play. The Ducks' first game was against the Edmonton Oilers, and no one was more nervous than Paul. This was the Northlands Coliseum, where his idol Wayne Gretzky had played so many of his amazing games. Although the Ducks lost 2–1, Paul impressed Edmonton's general manager, Glen Sather: "He's intelligent, aggressive, a very dedicated skater. He's going to be one of the new stars of the NHL."

In the next game, against the Winnipeg Jets (now the Phoenix Coyotes), Paul scored his first NHL goal. Over the course of that initial season, he stunned every team that saw him play for the first time. His own general manager, Jack Ferreira, continued to be impressed. "You look at him, and okay, he has great wheels and good hands. But those aren't his best assets. He has that sixth sense of knowing where everybody is, that great anticipation. There might be some things he'll do that you don't want him to do, but you have to let him go. You never want to control his creativeness."

An NHL superstar, Paul was brilliant in his first All-Star Game.

Paul led the Ducks in scoring that first season, and he was a finalist for the Calder Trophy, which is given every year to the NHL's best rookie. A big reason why he continued to succeed was that he always kept his personal life simple. In Anaheim he lived with Gary and Teri Frederick, an older couple who were friends of Ron Wilson, the Mighty Ducks' coach.

The 1995–96 season was important for Paul and the Mighty Ducks. He had put on a bit more weight over the summer, all added strength, and as a result he was more confident as a shooter. "I'd always been told growing up that I had a good shot," he told reporters. "I just never used it. I didn't have the strength. Now I'm stronger, my release is better, and the more I shoot, the more confidence I get."

Paul played on a line with Chad Kilger and Todd Krygier. Everyone called this the Special K Line because all their last names started with *K*. It was clear that Paul was one of the best young players in the league. He was chosen to compete in the All-Star Game in Boston, and even among the best of the best he was one of the stars. Standing beside him during the player introductions was Teemu Selanne of the Winnipeg Jets, another young superstar. Just a few weeks later Selanne was traded to Anaheim, and the Ducks had one of the best combinations in the world. "This will change the way I play the game," Paul said when he heard the good news. Selanne was just as fast as Paul and had as good a shot, and the two young stars played "in sync" perfectly. Every time they stepped on the ice together, Ducks fans went quackers.

Paul has learned to fight off checks and control the puck.

Anaheim finished the year with a much better record of 35–39–8, but missed the playoffs. Paul scored 50 goals and got more than 100 points. After only two years in the NHL, Paul was being compared to Wayne Gretzky by more and more people. He was truly the next Great One.

Now that Wayne Gretzky

has retired, the NHL

looks to Paul to take the

Great One's place.

CHAPTER FIVE
Disaster and Triumph

At the end of the 1995–96 season, Paul pulled a muscle in his groin. Over the summer, as he continued to exercise and prepare for the next year, his injury moved up to his stomach and got worse. He missed the first 12 games of 1996–97, and in that time the Ducks won just once. But when he started to play again, he and Teemu Selanne became the best two forwards in the league. "His weapons are his speed and his quickness," Selanne said of his friend and linemate. "He could easily become one of the greatest players of all time."

Paul was just as complimentary of Selanne: "It's so much fun playing the game when you know exactly what the other person's going to do." Together they helped lead the Ducks to their best season ever (36 wins and 85 points). Selanne finished the year with 109 points, and Paul had 99, even though he missed all those games at the start of the season.

Because the Ducks finished fourth in the Western Conference, they made it into the playoffs. They played the Phoenix Coyotes in the opening round. This was the first time the Ducks were going to compete for the Stanley Cup, and no one was more excited than Paul. He scored an important over-time goal in Game 5 that gave Anaheim a 3–2 lead in the series. It was just the kind of goal that thrilled his fans. Selanne saw Paul break out of his own end at full speed. He hit his linemate with a long, perfect pass, and Paul went in on Coyotes goalie Nikolai Khabibulin and blew a slap shot by him for the win.

In 1997 Paul won

the Lady Byng Trophy

for sportsmanship.

Two nights later the Ducks won 3–0, eliminating Phoenix for their first playoff series victory in their first postseason appearance.

Anaheim played Detroit next, but the Red Wings were too good and the Ducks lost in four straight games. Detroit went on to win the Stanley Cup, so Paul now knew what it would take to beat the best team in the league. As he looked to the summer, he was excited to prepare for the next season, not just because of the NHL but because he would be returning to Nagano, Japan, to represent Canada at the 1998 Olympics.

However, the 1997–98 season didn't begin or end the way Paul had hoped. It started badly when he and the Ducks couldn't agree on a new contract, and he missed the first 32 games of the season. As a goodwill gesture, Paul donated his salary for those games to charity, an amount that was almost $2 million.

Soon after he started playing again, Paul was officially named to the Canadian Olympic team, which consisted entirely of NHL players for the first time. He was honored by the announcement and couldn't wait until February when the Olympics began.

Dave King, a former coach of Canada's teams in the Olympics, had also been coach and adviser to Japan's national teams. He saw the chance for big things to come out of Paul's participation in Nagano. "Paul probably doesn't fully realize his importance to Japan," King said. "He's the most revered NHL player there. Sure, they like Wayne Gretzky and Raymond Bourque, but because of Paul's heritage, he's the guy the focus will be on. There's not a lot of hockey in Japan, but they know the game. The Japanese see themselves in Paul. He's skilled and courageous. His presence in Nagano could motivate a lot of Japanese kids to play the sport."

Disaster struck, however, on February 1, 1998, just two weeks

He Juggles, He Scores

During the contract disagreement between NHL owners and players in 1994, Paul Kariya had nothing to do while there was no hockey. One day, when he was at the airport waiting for a flight, he bought a book called *Lessons from the Art of Juggling*. "It's really about more than learning how to juggle," he explains. "I followed the lessons, though. I can do the trick where you eat an apple while you're juggling, and I can juggle behind my back. If it gives you just that split second more of coordination, it's something you have."

before the Olympics. In a game against Chicago, Paul was in front of the net. He knocked a rebound in for a goal, but in the same instant Blackhawks defenseman Gary Suter cross-checked him hard to the head. Paul got up slowly and left the ice. He didn't play again for seven months.

When he got to the bench after the hit, Paul thought he was just shaken up a bit. But his doctor soon realized that Paul was seriously injured. In the days that followed, he had painful headaches that wouldn't go away. He got extremely tired even when he walked across his living room. He was dizzy and felt sick for long periods of time. Paul had suffered a concussion.

A concussion occurs when a violent collision forces the brain to hit the inside of the skull. The movement shocks the brain and leaves the person in a great deal of pain. That's what happened to Paul. He couldn't remember anything. He couldn't exercise at all without feeling sick. He couldn't function as a person let alone as a hockey player. Paul's dream of playing in Nagano had been destroyed, and the millions of people in Canada and Japan who had wanted to see him play were disappointed.

X MARKS THE SPOT

At the Mighty Ducks' practice rink, Paul Kariya has marked a small *X* on one section of the boards. He stands back about 20 feet (six meters) from the spot and takes passes from a teammate. He quickly controls the puck, and *bam*, hits the *X*. Another pass, and *bam!* Right on the *X*. Gradually he moves from a simple wrist shot to a onetime snap shot. *Bam!* Another hit. Then he tries his slap shot. *Bam! Bam! Bam!* That's why he has one of the hardest, most accurate shots in the league.

Paul had to rest and wait for his concussion symptoms to go away before he could begin to train again. His friend Eric Lindros phoned him to wish him well and suggested he try acupuncture, a Chinese practice that uses needles in various parts of the body to relieve pain. He also hired a special cook to prepare healthy meals, and by the time training camp arrived for the new season, he was completely fit.

To make sure he stayed healthy, Paul had a special helmet made, with extra padding inside and a tighter chin strap so the helmet would never be loose. He also started wearing a mouth guard and did strength exercises to improve his neck muscles and his flexibility.

In 1998–99, everything was perfect for the full season. Paul and Teemu Selanne were again the best two players in the league, and they both registered 100-point seasons. In the playoffs, though, the Ducks lost to Detroit in four games again. Paul missed the last one because of a broken foot he suffered when he bravely blocked a shot in Game 3. Although he was disappointed by the quick end to the season, he saw the bright side of life at all times.

Captain Kariya hopes to lead his team to a Stanley Cup one day.

As the NHL heads into the 21st century and the new millennium, the league continues to count on Paul Kariya to be one of its greatest superstars in the rink and one of its finest gentlemen off the ice. Not yet in the prime years of his career, Paul will play for Canada at the 2002 Olympics and will whiz up and down the ice faster than anyone else for many years to come.

1993–94	National Team	23	7	34	41	2
1994	World Championships	8	5	7	12	2
1994	Olympics	8	3	4	7	2
1996	World Championships	8	4	3	7	2
Totals		**68**	**24**	**62**	**86**	**12**

STATISTICS

British Columbia Junior Hockey League (BCJHL)

Regular Season

Year	Team	GP	G	A	P	PIM
1990–91	Penticton	54	45	67	112	8
1991–92	Penticton	40	46	86	132	18
Totals		**94**	**91**	**153**	**244**	**26**

National Collegiate Athletic Association Hockey East

Regular Season

Year	Team	GP	G	A	P	PIM
1992–93	U of Maine	36	24	69	93	12
1993–94	U of Maine	12	8	16	24	4
Totals		**48**	**32**	**85**	**117**	**16**

Canadian International Hockey

Year	Event	GP	G	A	P	PIM
1992	World Juniors	6	1	1	2	2
1993	World Juniors	7	2	6	8	2
1993	World Championships	8	2	7	9	0

National Hockey League (NHL)

Regular Season

Year	Team	GP	G	A	P	PIM
1994–95	Anaheim	47	18	21	39	4
1995–96	Anaheim	82	50	58	108	20
1996–97	Anaheim	69	44	55	99	6
1997–98	Anaheim	22	17	14	31	23
1998–99	Anaheim	82	39	62	101	40
1999–2000	Anaheim	74	42	44	86	24
Totals		**376**	**210**	**254**	**464**	**117**

Playoffs

Year	Team	GP	G	A	P	PIM
1997	Anaheim	11	7	6	13	4
1999	Anaheim	3	1	3	4	0
Totals		**14**	**8**	**9**	**17**	**4**

Key

GP = Games Played   G = Goals   A = Assists
P = Points   PIM = Penalties in Minutes